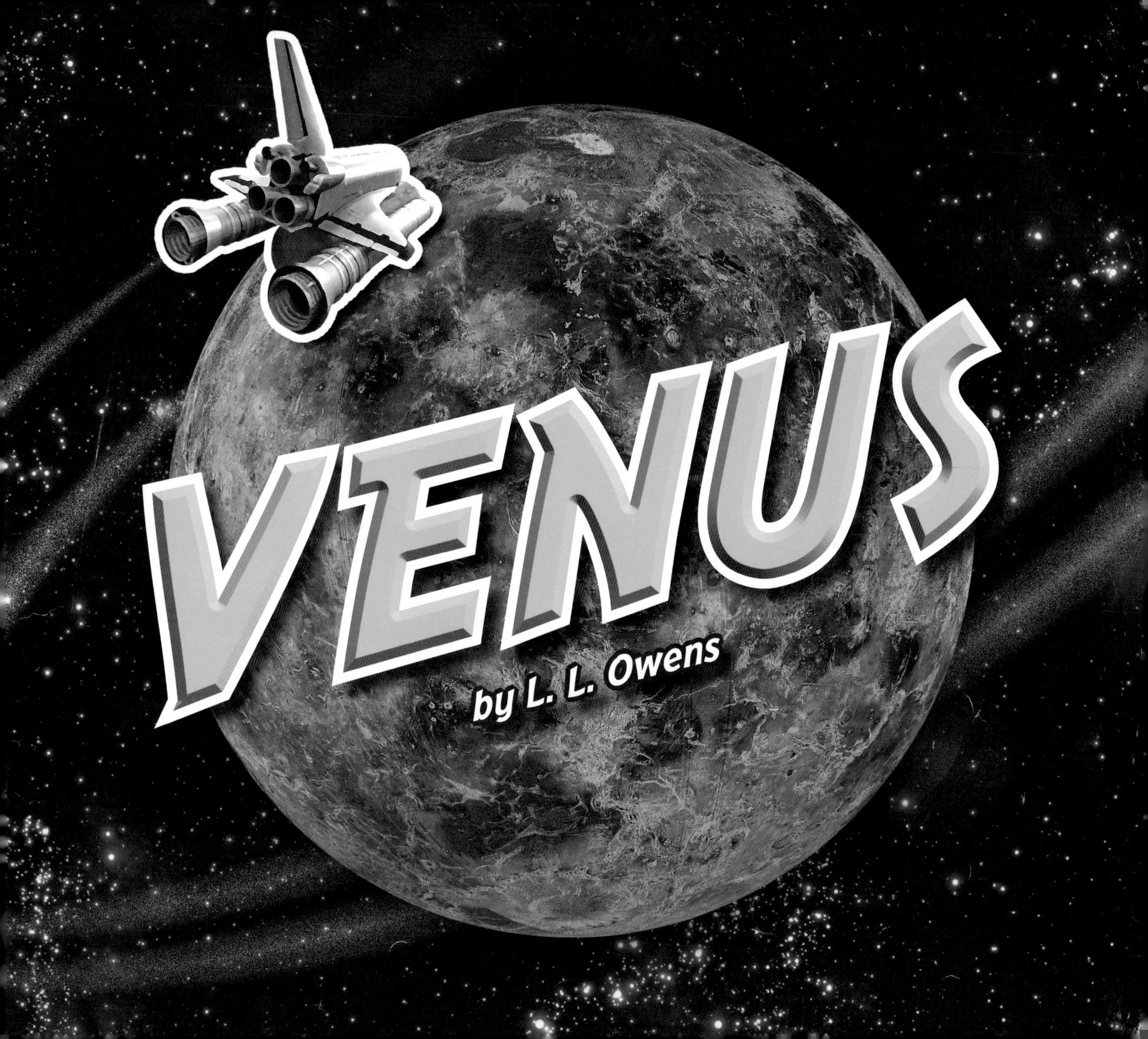
VENUS
by L. L. Owens

Published by The Child's World®
1980 Lookout Drive • Mankato, MN 56003-1705
800-599-READ • www.childsworld.com

ACKNOWLEDGMENTS
The Child's World®: Mary Berendes, Publishing Director
The Design Lab: Design and production
Red Line Editorial: Editorial direction

PHOTO CREDITS
NASA/courtesy of nasaimages.org, cover, 1, 3, 4, 6, 8, 10, 12, 17, 19, 21, 25, 26, 31, 32; George Frey/AP Images, 5; NASA/courtesy of nasaimages.org/The Design Lab, 6, 7, 9; R. V. Bulck/iStockphoto, 11; NASA/NSSDC/Jet Propulsion Laboratory (NASA-JPL), 13, 29; NASA/NSSDC/Catalog of Spaceborne Imaging, 15, 27; Jared Leeds/AP Images, 23

LIBRARY OF CONGRESS CATALOGING-IN-PUBLICATION DATA
Owens, L. L.
Venus / by L.L. Owens.
p. cm.
Includes bibliographical references and index.
ISBN 978-1-60954-390-7 (library bound : alk. paper)
1. Venus (Planet)—Juvenile literature. I. Title.
QB621.O94 2010
523.42–dc22
2010040462

Printed in the United States of America
Mankato, MN
May, 2012
PA02138

ON THE COVER
The colors in this image of Venus show high and low points on the planet's surface.

Table of Contents

Venus and the Solar System

Try looking in the western sky after sunset. Do you see a bright, shining object? That's Venus! Venus looks brighter than any star in the night sky.

Venus is one of our space neighbors in the **solar system**. At the center of our solar system is the sun. Planets go around, or **orbit**, the sun.

Fun Fact

Even though it is a planet, one nickname for Venus is Evening Star. But Venus is also called Morning Star. At certain times of the year, you can see Venus in the eastern sky before sunrise.

Venus (top left) is seen over Provo, Utah, in 2005. Jupiter is to the right of the moon.

SUN

Mercury

Venus

Earth

Mars

Ceres

Jupiter

PLANET NUMBER: Venus is the second planet from the sun.

DISTANCE FROM SUN: 67 million miles (108 million km)

SIZE: The distance around Venus's middle is about 23,627 miles (38,024 km). That's almost as long as 50 million baseball bats placed end to end!

OUR SOLAR SYSTEM: Our solar system has eight planets and five **dwarf planets**. Pluto used to be called a planet. But in 2006, scientists decided to call it a dwarf planet instead. Scientists hope to discover even more dwarf planets in our solar system!

Our Solar System
Saturn
Uranus
Neptune
Pluto
Haumea
Makemake
Eris
Planet
Dwarf Planet

While orbiting the sun, a planet spins like a top. Imagine a line going through the planet from top to bottom. That's the planet's **axis**. Each planet spins, or rotates, on its axis. One rotation equals one day. Think of one day on a planet as the time from one sunrise to the next sunrise.

Fun Fact

Venus spins in the opposite direction from Earth and most other planets. On Venus, the sun rises in the west and sets in the east.

An axis runs through the center of a planet. The planet spins on the axis.

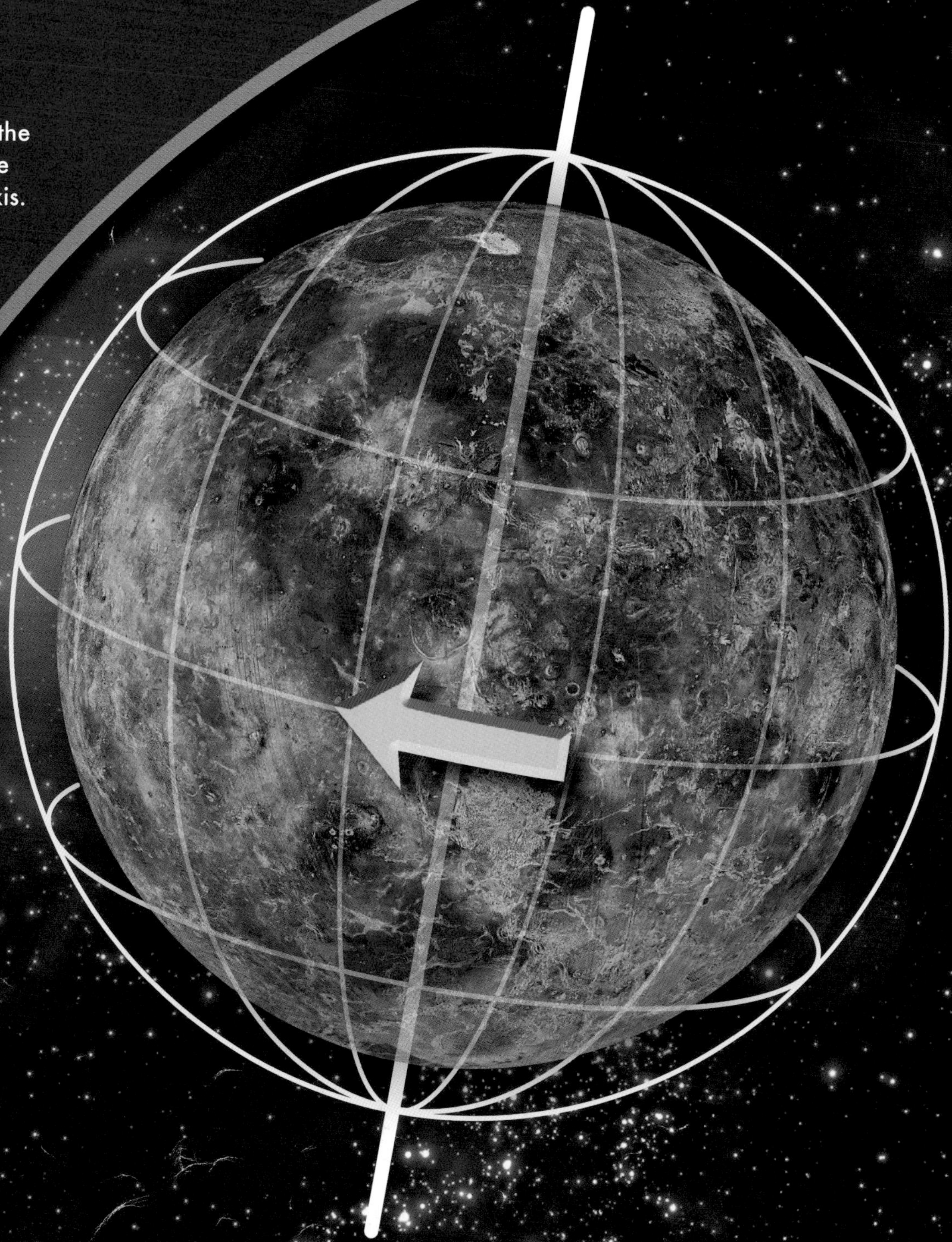

Venus rotates very slowly—once every 243 Earth days. An Earth day is 24 hours. That means one day on Venus is 5,832 hours!

A year is the time it takes for a planet to travel around the sun once. Venus's orbit around the sun takes about 225 Earth days. It takes Earth about 365 days to orbit the sun.

Fun Fact

Venus is also called Earth's twin. The two planets are similar in size, but they are very different.

Venus was named after the Roman goddess of love.

A Hard, Rocky Planet

Venus is a **terrestrial** planet. It is rocky and hard. It has mountains, canyons, and volcanoes. Other planets are made of **gas**—they have no hard surface.

There are two types of planets.

TERRESTRIAL PLANETS (mostly rock) are close to the sun. They are: Mercury, Venus, Earth, and Mars.

GAS GIANTS (mostly gas and liquid) are farther from the sun. They are: Jupiter, Saturn, Uranus, and Neptune.

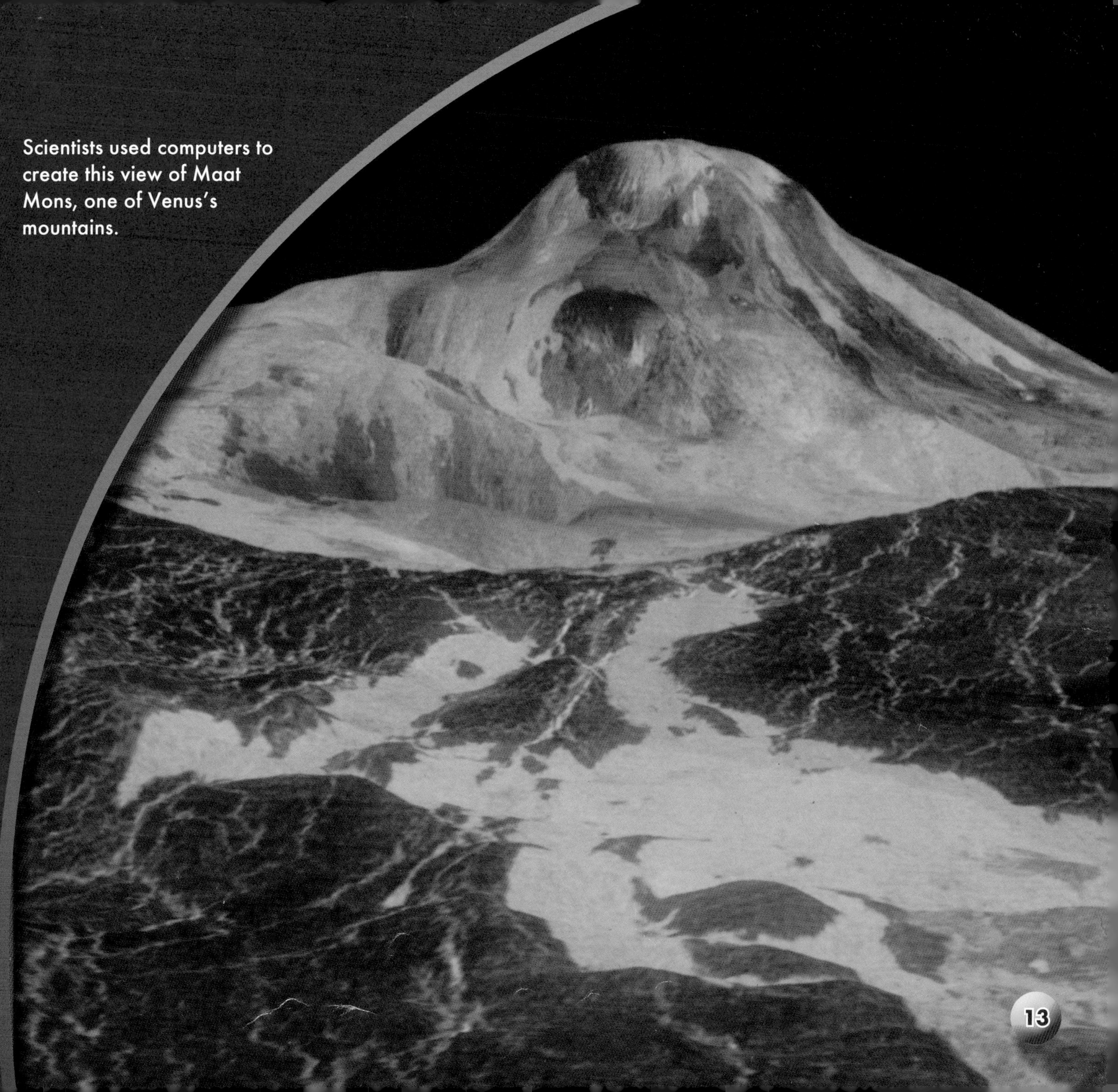

Scientists used computers to create this view of Maat Mons, one of Venus's mountains.

A Closer Look

In space, Venus looks like a big yellow ball. The surface includes some flat areas, or plains. It's also dotted with **craters**. Millions of years ago, **asteroids** slammed into Venus. These fiery masses of rock dented Venus's rocky surface, carving out craters.

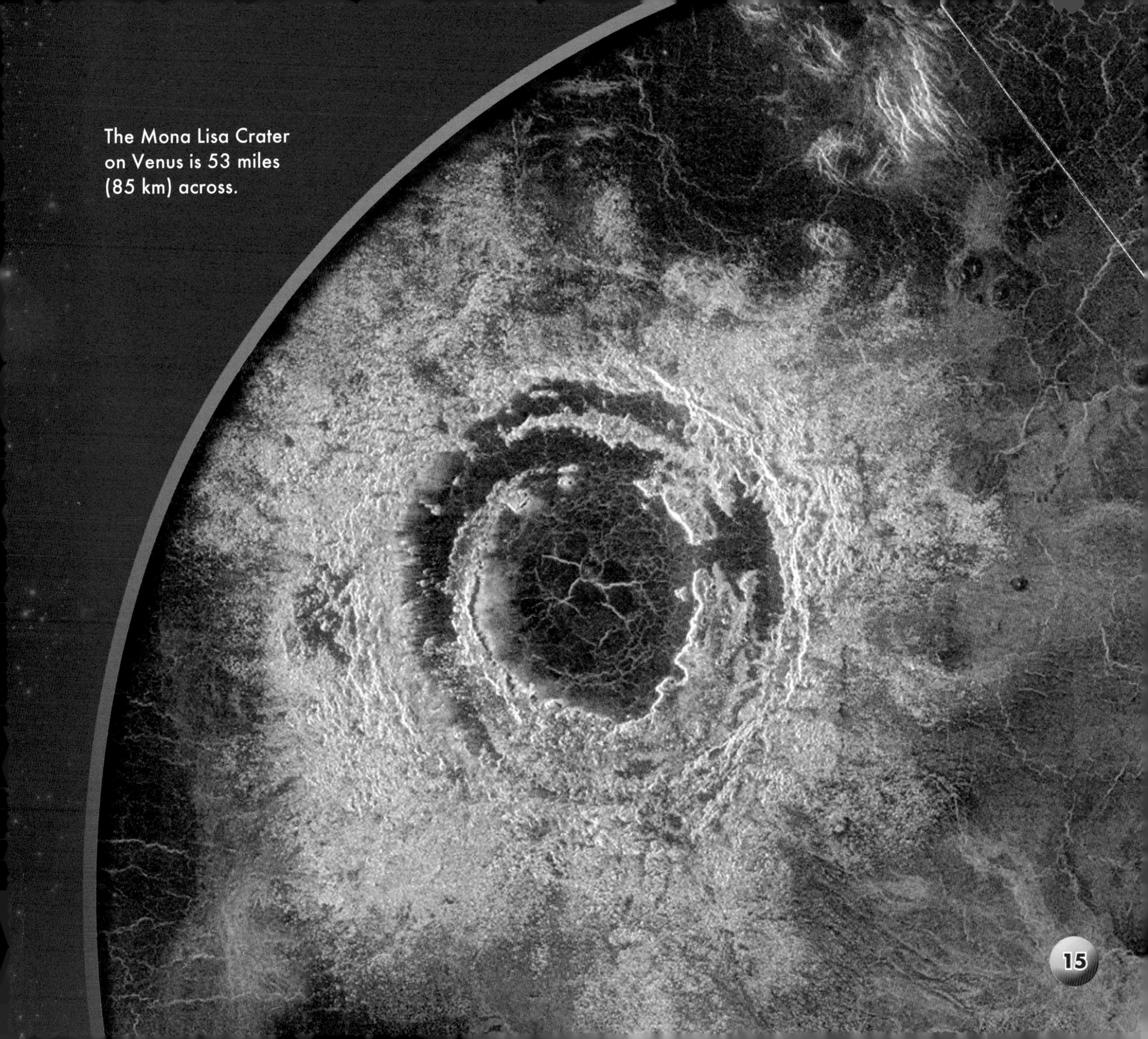

The Mona Lisa Crater on Venus is 53 miles (85 km) across.

Venus has two large highland areas. They are landmasses like Earth's continents. Ishtar Terra is about the size of Australia. Aphrodite Terra is similar in size to South America.

Maxwell Montes is the highest mountain range on Venus. The peak is 7 miles (11 km) high. That's higher than Earth's tallest mountain!

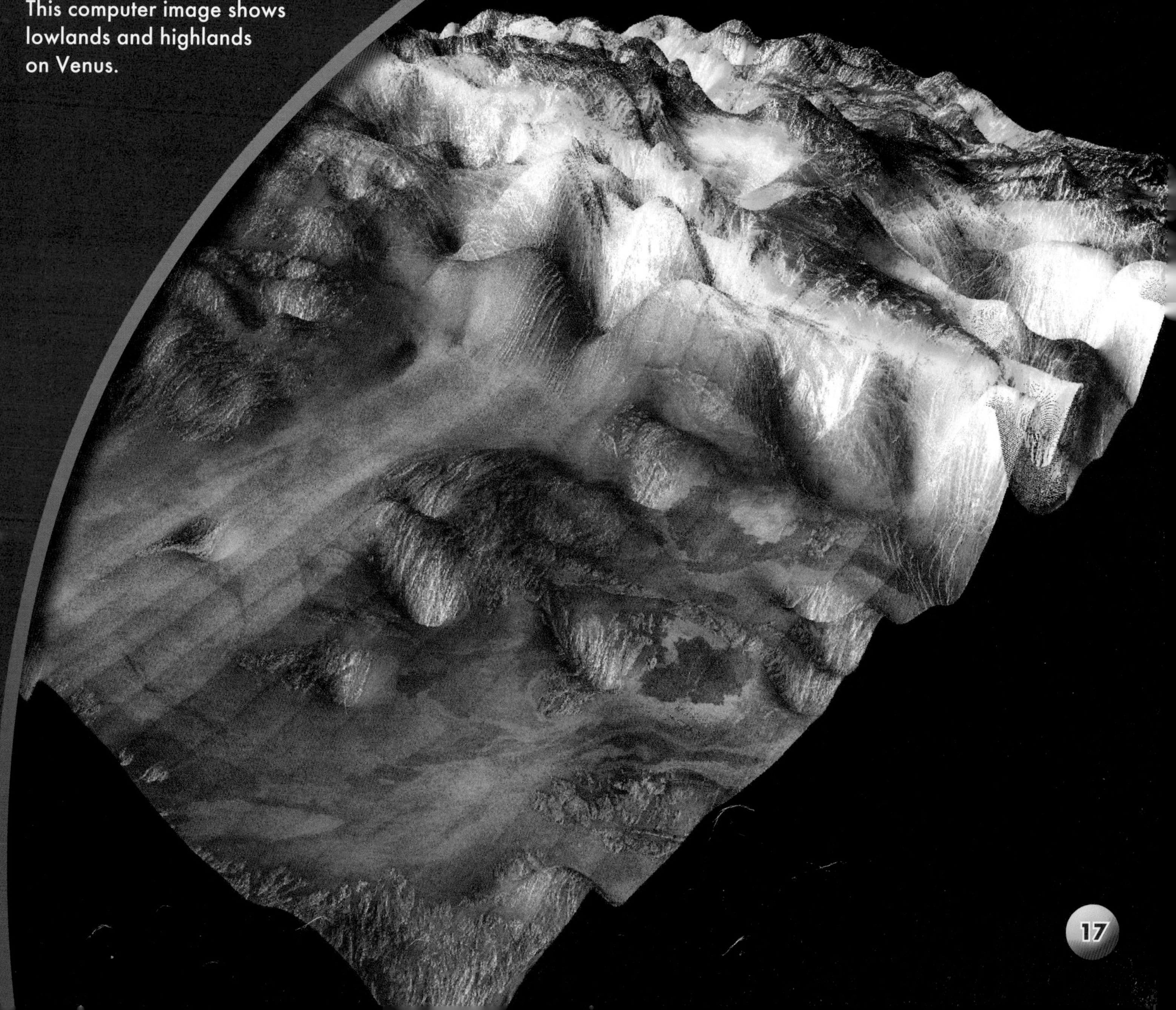

This computer image shows lowlands and highlands on Venus.

Weather and Water

A planet's **atmosphere** is the layer of gas around it. Earth's atmosphere is the air that we breathe. Venus's atmosphere is made up of thick, **toxic** clouds. The rain they make is poisonous to living things. You would not be able to breathe on Venus.

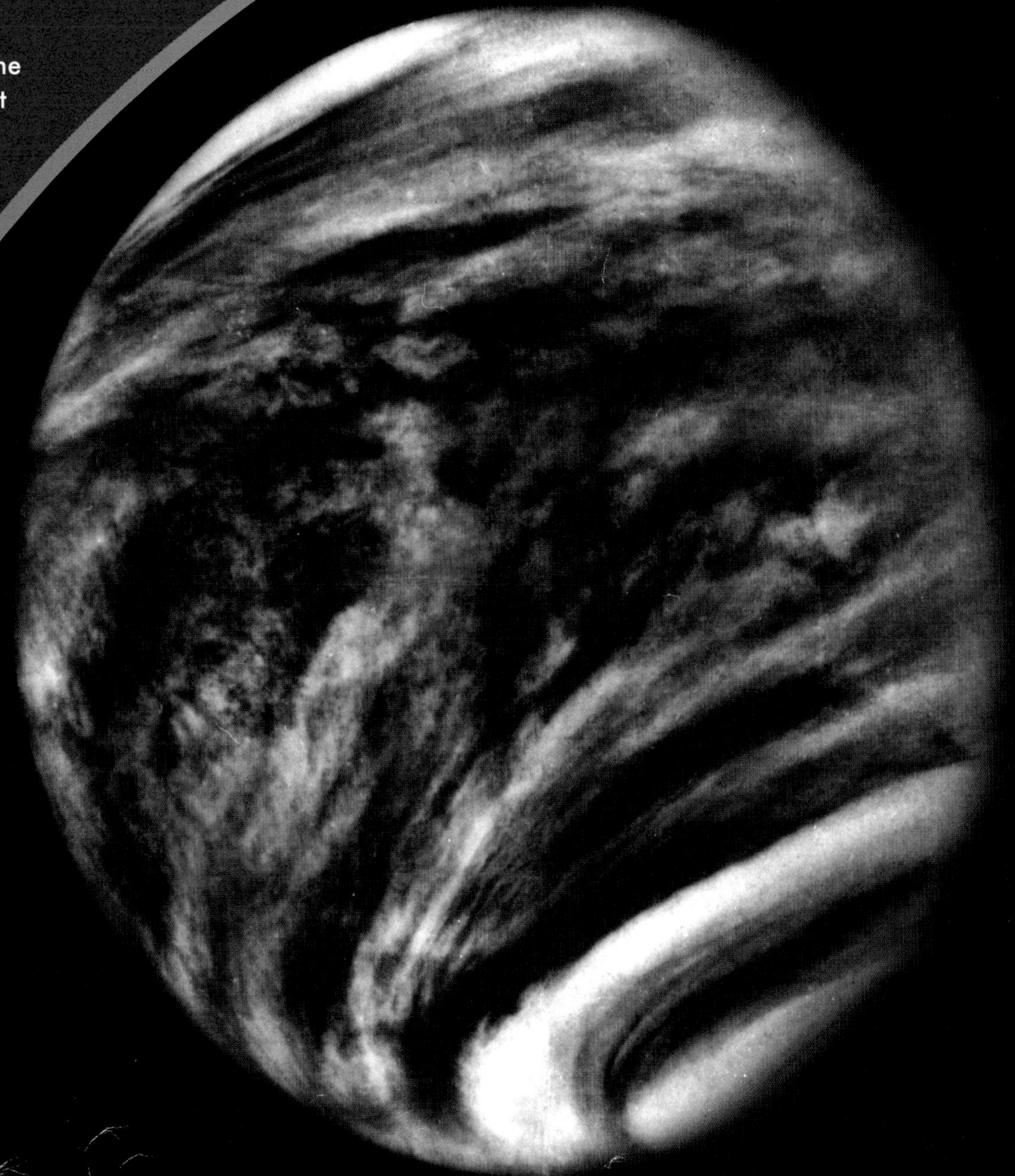

This image of Venus's clouds was taken by the *Mariner 10* spacecraft in 1974.

Venus is the hottest planet in our solar system. The surface temperature on Venus is 870°F (465°C). That's more than six times hotter than Earth's hottest desert!

Venus stays hot from morning through night, too. Its blanket of heavy clouds traps in the heat.

Venus is covered in
thick clouds.

Scientists have looked for water on Venus. All life as we know it needs water. But Venus is extremely dry. The sun's heat would boil away any water on its surface. And scientists have found no traces of water in its deep craters.

A student uses a **telescope** to view Venus.

Exploring the Planet

How do scientists know about Venus? No one has ever walked on the planet. But scientists have sent spacecraft to explore it. The spacecraft map the surface and collect temperature **data**.

Several spacecraft have landed on Venus long enough to take photographs. Windows made of diamonds protected the camera lenses from the heat.

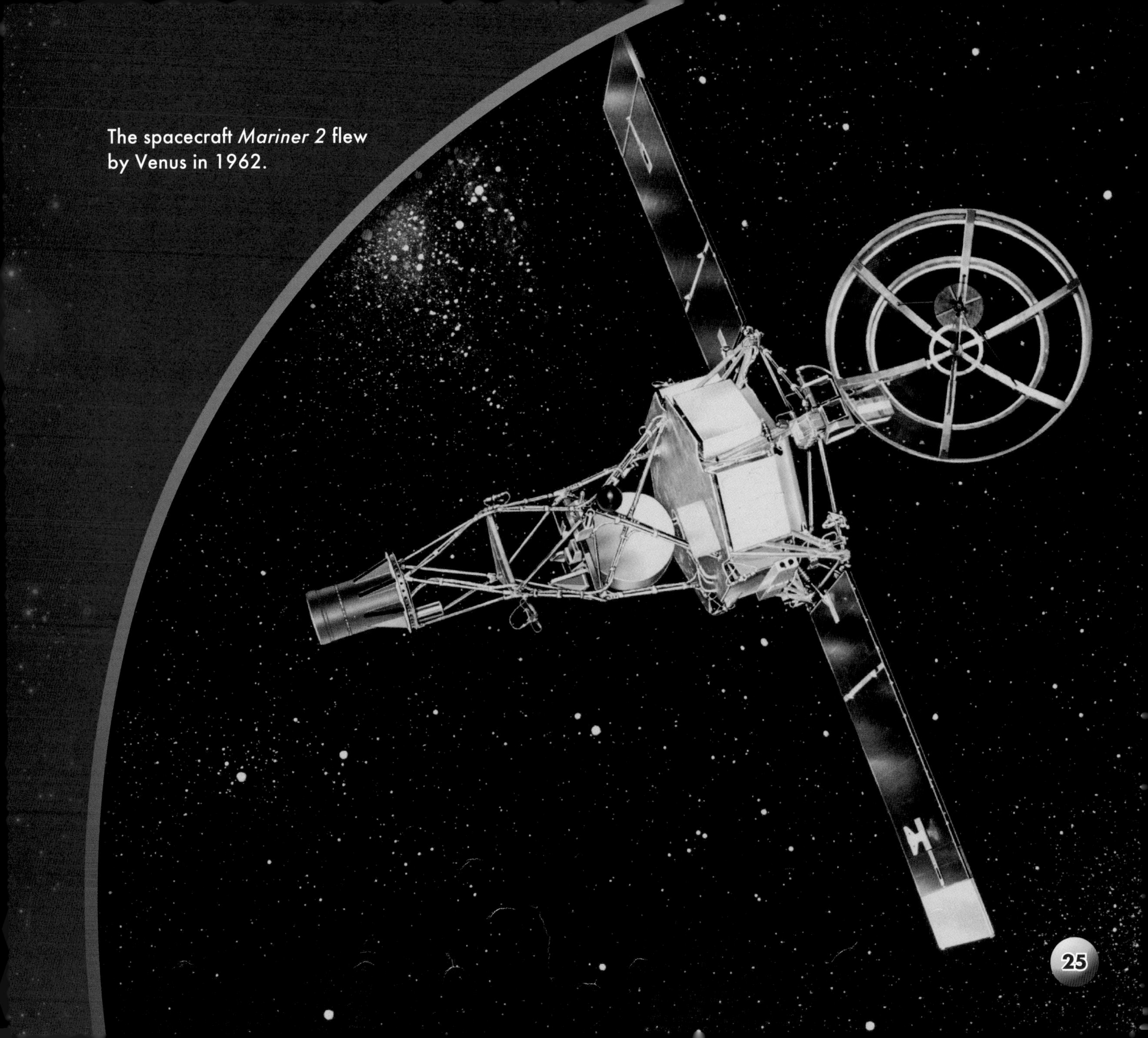

The spacecraft *Mariner 2* flew by Venus in 1962.

In 2010, NASA scientists made an exciting discovery. Data showed there might have been recent **lava** flows on Venus. That means volcanoes might still be active on the planet! In our solar system, only a few other planets and moons are thought to have active volcanoes.

Fun Fact

NASA stands for the National Aeronautics and Space Administration. It is a US agency that studies space and the planets.

The *Magellan* spacecraft took this image showing lava flows on Venus.

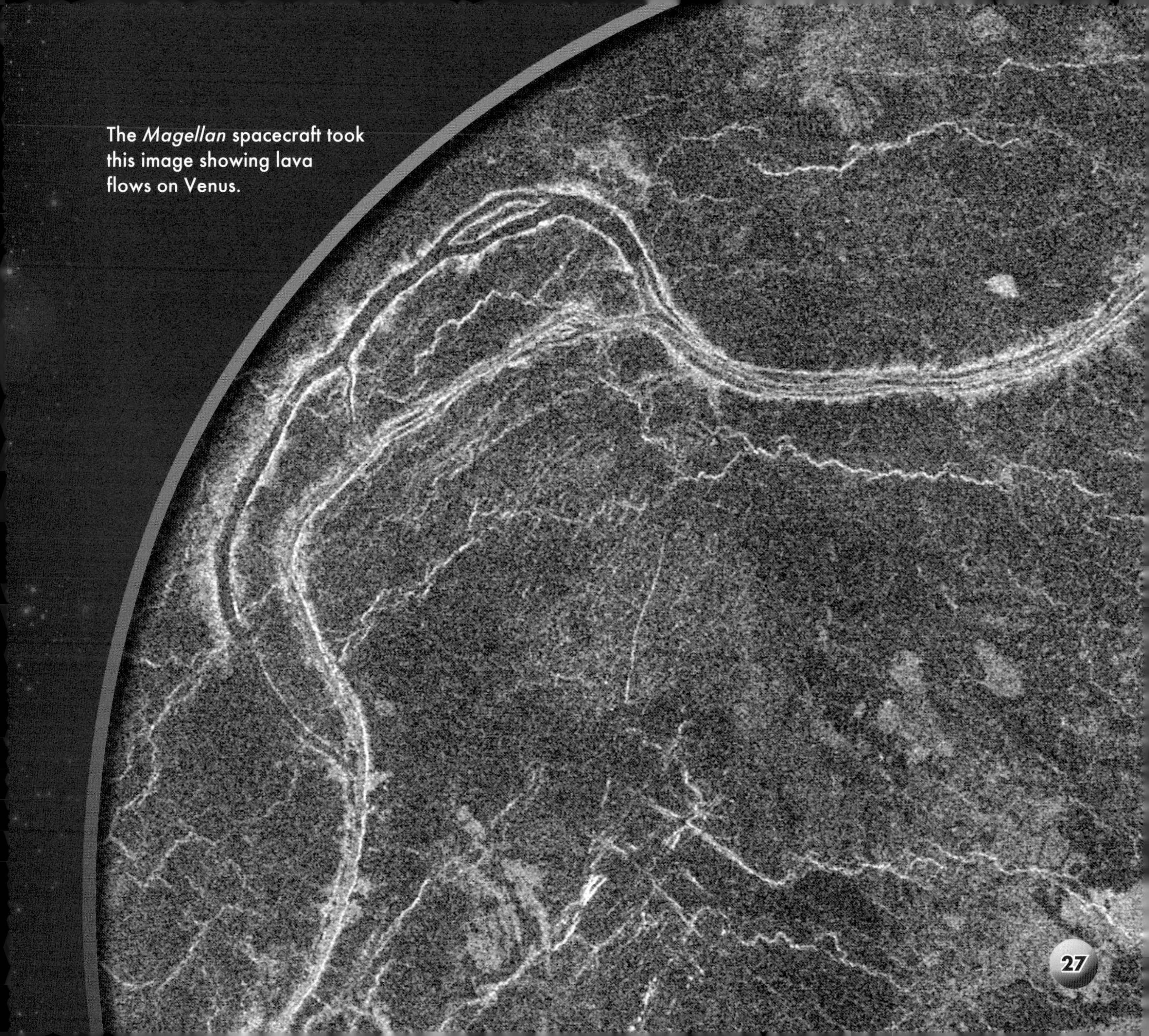

Investigating the lava flows will help scientists understand the planet's core, or inside, and how the planet works. NASA hopes to get more data about the planet's atmosphere, surface, and history. New findings will help us better understand Venus and how our solar system came to be.

This image of Venus was colored blue to show the planet's cloud markings.

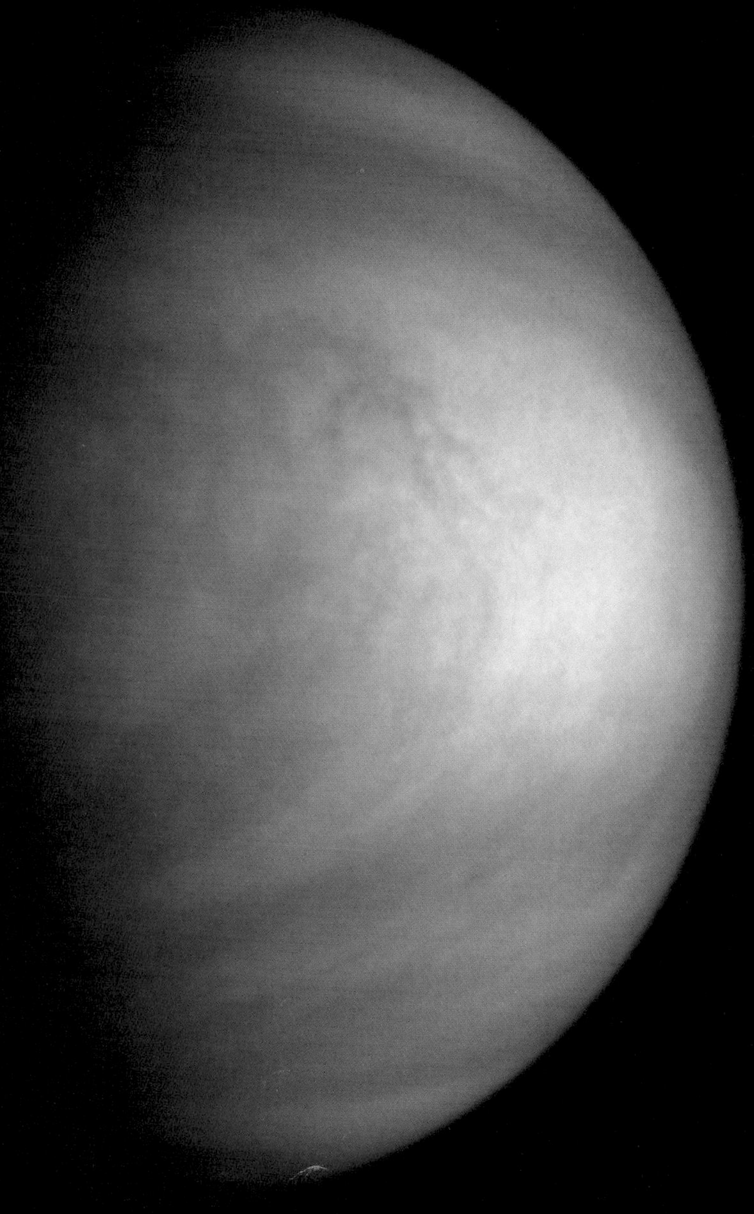

GLOSSARY

asteroids (ASS-tuh-roidz): Asteroids are rocks that orbit the sun. Asteroids slammed into Venus and caused deep craters on the planet's surface.

atmosphere (AT-muhss-fihr): An atmosphere is the mixture of gases around a planet or a star. Venus's atmosphere is made of thick, poisonous clouds.

axis (AK-siss): An axis is an imaginary line that runs through the center of a planet or a moon. Venus rotates on its axis.

craters (KRAY-turz): Craters are large areas on the surface of a moon or a planet that dip down, like bowls. Venus has craters dotting its surface.

data (DAY-tuh): Data are facts, figures, and other information. Scientists hope to gather more data about Venus.

dwarf planets (DWORF PLAN-itz): Dwarf planets are round bodies in space that orbit the sun, are not moons, and are not large enough to clear away their paths around the sun. Dwarf planets often have similar objects that orbit near them.

gas (GASS): A gas is a substance that moves around freely and can spread out. Some planets are made mostly of gas.

lava (LAH-vuh): Lava is molten, or melted, rock from a volcano or a deep crack in land. Scientists discovered that there might have been recent lava flows on Venus.

orbit (OR-bit): To orbit is to travel around another body in space, often in an oval path. Planets orbit the sun.

solar system (SOH-lur SISS-tum): Our solar system is made up of the sun, eight planets and their moons, and smaller bodies that orbit the sun. Venus is the second planet from the sun in our solar system.

telescope (TEL-uh-skope): A telescope is a tool that makes faraway objects appear closer. Venus can be seen without a telescope.

terrestrial (tuh-RESS-tree-uhl): Terrestrial describes planets that have firm land, like Earth. Venus is a terrestrial planet.

toxic (TOK-sik): To be toxic is to be poisonous. Venus's atmosphere has toxic clouds.

FURTHER INFORMATION

BOOKS

Birch, Robin. *Venus*. New York: Chelsea House, 2008.

Landau, Elaine. *Venus*. New York: Children's Press, 2008.

Trammel, Howard K. *The Solar System*. New York: Children's Press, 2010.

WEB SITES

Visit our Web site for links about Venus: **childsworld.com/links**

Note to Parents, Teachers, and Librarians: We routinely verify our Web links to make sure they are safe and active sites. So encourage your readers to check them out!

INDEX

ABOUT THE AUTHOR

L. L. Owens has been writing books for children since 1998. She writes both fiction and nonfiction and especially loves helping kids explore the world around them.